BE
UNAPOLOGETICALLY
YOU

A SELF LOVE GUIDE
FOR WOMEN OF COLOR

ADELINE BIRD

COURONNE PUBLISHING
WINNIPEG, MANITOBA

Couronne Publishing Inc.
1-3377 Pembina Highway, Winnipeg, MB. Canada. R3V1A2
Info@couronnepublishing.com
www.couronnepublishing.com

Ordering Information:
Quantity sales. Special discounts are available on quantity pur-chases by corporations, associations, and others. For details, contact the "Special Sales Department" at the address above.

BE UNAPLOLOGETICALLY YOU: A SELF-LOVE GUIDE FOR WOMEN OF COLOR –Adeline Bird -1st edition.
ISBN 978-0-9948637-8-2

Wherever women and girls are, there is magic...

For the future, Maleena, Asia, Saqqara, Zendaya, Sunrah, Suntha, Katelyn & Skyla.

With Love, Style & Grace,

Adeline Bird
Host/Founder of Soul Unexpected

Aaah! Yes!! Finally!!! This book is exactly what we all need for our SOULS! I received unexpected insights and a gentle reminder of how important and deserving it is to LOVE yourself first.

Welcome to Adeline's incredible world of 'Be Unapologetically YOU'. I recommend this book to anyone who is willing and ready to explore their true self.

Adeline has powerfully captured what we all desire knowing that it starts with you first.

—

Delia Joseph, CPC
CEO and Founder of
Improveology Lifestyle Coaching
www.improveologylifestylecoaching.com

CONTENTS

....

OPENING TREATMENT

SELF-LOVE WILL REQUIRE YOU TO OPEN UP.

GIVE LIFE TO YOUR WORTH AND EVERYTHING YOU DESERVE. EXPOSE YOURSELF TO THE MOST IMPORTANT RELATIONSHIP YOU WILL EVER HAVE, WHICH IS YOURSELF.

EMBRACE THE VULNERABILITY, SET CLEAR, CONSCIENCE AND LOVING INTENTIONS TO YOUR SOUL.

ASK YOURSELF, "HOW DO I WANT TO FEEL ABOUT MYSELF?"

ANSWER WITH EVERY CELL THAT'S BEEN WAITING FOR THIS MOMENT, THE MOMENT OF BEING ACKNOWLEDGED, ADORED, CARED FOR AND LOVED.

LEAN IN.
GET FOCUSED.
HONOR YOURSELF.

INTRODUCTION

Self-love has been a buzzword in self-help circles for many years. Everyone has heard of it but do you really know what it means? And even more importantly, do you know how to achieve it?

A very basic definition of self-love is how you feel about yourself. A sense of regard and appreciation for your true being. People who lack self-love struggle in life are more prone to mental health issues and generally do not reach their true potential. They can also be difficult to be around.

However, there is hope. This book is designed to help you discover self-love and unlock all the benefits that come with it. I will give you keys to boosting your self-love. There are tips, tricks and exercises to help you remember how valuable you are as a person.

This book is designed to help you evolve into your version of self-love and is specifically written for women of color. As a woman of color, I understand that we face unique experiences and challenges that, one way or the other, affect how we feel about ourselves. We face experiences based on systematic oppression, racism, classism, sexism and other unique experiences.

There is no question that having to relive some of these experiences on a daily basis begins to take a toll on how you feel about yourself and the world around you. In my experience, the way to deal with such topics and experiences can be through learning how to love oneself. When you begin to learn how to love yourself and view yourself in a positive way, that can start to reflect and manifest into the real world.

I'm here to show you that no matter what negative things you may have experienced it is not who you are. You are not inadequate because you are too brown or your hair is too nappy, you are love. Perhaps like me you come from a family of gang members, drug abuse or even violence. I need you to understand this is not who you are, you are love. This is why learning to love yourself is crucial. Keep in mind it does not happen overnight. It's a journey that will evolve as you grow.

As a little girl I remember feeling ashamed for having a head full of hair that felt like no one could manage. Keep in mind I'm mixed, raised by a First Nations woman who knew nothing about black hair. My sister and I ran around with the most unmanageable and wildest hair in the entire neighborhood. As an eight-year-old girl, I felt ashamed and out of place. I remember sitting in my classroom and my friend Shelly walking in with her long luscious hair. I remember feeling ashamed and envious and wondering, "why can't my hair be like that?" "Why do I look different from all the pretty girls?"

At the age of 15, it began to occur to me that my shame was rooted in the imagery that I had been exposed to all my life. From picture books to magazines, the images and the message of what this standard beauty is, is slim, 5'8", blonde hair, pale skinned women. I started to question myself and I started to ask the question, "Where does my beauty lie?" This is a question that I carried for years. It wasn't until I discovered personal development which became my anchor to self-love that I began to see the inkling of an answer.

As you're going through this book, I want you to keep in mind that there is a difference between self-love and ego but they both work for and with each other. I once read a response to a question posed to Deepak Chopra on his website on the difference between the ego and self-love. His response eloquently describes what I mean. For most people, self-esteem and ego defense amount to the same thing. In that scenario feeling good about yourself is feeling good about your egoistic personality.

However, true self-esteem is based on direct experience of your core consciousness, your higher self which lies beyond your ego. That sense of inner well-being comes from knowing your spiritual self. Provides a real sense of esteem that has nothing to do with one's personality or ego. Your real self doesn't derive its sense of value from your thoughts and behavior nor does it care what others think of you. It cannot feel embarrassed, resentful, humiliated or proud. The esteem of higher self is simply the recognition of pure awareness.

Are you ready to unlock and release all that does not serve you and step fully into your authentic, most creative and soulful self? As with all things, there is a price to pay. You as an individual need to open yourself up to understand what has defined you and accept the position of vulnerability that opening up places you in. The opportunities that open up to you are endless. Inspiration, liberation and authenticity are some of the benefits that you will gain when you discover self-love.

ADELINE BIRD

SECTION ONE

....

SELF LOVE AS A CONSCIOUS AND SOULFUL ACT

ONE

....

KNOW THY HISTORY

Self-love was first introduced to me through my journey into personal development but it wasn't always a rosy process. Along the way I stumbled. Personal development gave me some good tools, but I became frustrated with the process, because the message and tools did not match what I was seeing in my reality and the world I live in. It felt like something was missing.

There is a core, undeniable truth that was not being told. In the search for this truth, I had to overcome some of the more unpleasant mistruths that we are bombarded with every day and accept that my journey to self-love might not be found in the typical places.

I can't even begin to explain how discouraging it is to go online, or log onto your social media and continuously see images of black men and women being brutalized or killed on camera for the world to see, or to hear that another aboriginal woman or girl has gone missing or was murdered. What's even more heart wrenching is reading the comment sections on these issues as the negativity, ingrained stereotypes and blatant hatred are perpetuating the problem. I began to ask myself, how I can remain positive when all these horrible things are happening to people who look like me and come from a similar background as me. I started to feel bitter and resentful towards everyone and anything that had to do with personal development because it felt like a white man's privilege.

I love me some Tony Robbins but being told thinking positive at all times is the key to personal development and hearing quotes like "What people can do is very different from what they will do." are hard to comprehend when you're up against a system designed to keep women and people of color oppressed. Let's take Trayvon Martin or Tina Fontaine as two of many possible examples. Both of them and many, thousands more were not given a chance to be. Their situations had little to do with choosing to be positive or what they were willing to do. Often personal development starts on an assumption of safety. For many of us (including Tina Fontaine and Trayvon Martin) fears are justified as the systems in place constantly fail. It was not a huge leap to question myself, wondering if I might be next. This is a real question for many people of color. These stories are so heartbreaking it is hard not to feel hopeless. Despite all the negative stories and narratives that surrounded me, I did my best to remain positive in my own way. Instead of buying into the sick injustice that is accepted by the masses, I started to take the time to understand my history, the roots of my ancestors.

Knowing most people do not understand or acknowledge that the history we learn does not teach truth is very angering. That we have allowed our society to be programmed without knowledge or consent is a scary thing. A slave-like, segregated society is still very prevalent and it is being overlooked by the masses because we now live in a flash video world where news is entertainment and the focus quickly moves to the next pressing matter. Sometimes I feel that the stereotypes against my heritage are put into place to keep people from realizing we are all being misled.

Perpetuating the conflict among ourselves stops us from looking at the real problem.

By reminding and accentuating cultural differences people are stereotyping and segregating instead of focusing on humanity. There is a culture of division being encouraged and it is fueled by online, anonymous hatred. Mainstream media is encouraging the message rather than embracing diversity and finding similarities. It is amazing what is ignored just to fuel a specific agenda. Instead of allowing myself to buy into the negativity I delved deeper into the truths of my ancestors.

Being both of African and First Nations decent, when I started to look at my roots I found information beyond mainstream narratives, media, text books, accepted history, etc. In doing so I began to question previous assumptions and started to wonder who my ancestors were before colonialism. This wonder took me on a magnificent journey into understanding not only my ancestors, but myself. I came across knowledge of the legendary kingdoms of Egypt and Kush, the beginning of civilization. These ancient kingdoms were using technology and systems that we don't fully understand today, with vast, accurate scientific data. I also learned that

Turtle Island (North America) before European contact was rich of natural resources. There were cities and towns bigger than London or Rome made of the best materials ever seen that are still standing today. Also there are writings that are thousands of years old carved in stone in Ireland, Egypt and North America that match. There is a strong connection in our very early history that is shared with all cultures though few care to explore. Learning this itself liberated me. To know, I am more than just a descendant of slaves or savages took the way I saw myself and how I love myself to a whole other level.

The implications of this knowledge resonated throughout my whole life. Knowing my history and learning about my ancestors instilled in me a confidence that I am more than the stereotypes assigned to me. As well, from a health perspective, roots and history are very important. My physical and mental health is partially derived from genetics, from the lifestyle of my ancestors, for generations past. Studying, more closely my heritage and the lives of my ancestors, gave me insight into my own personal health. As well, instead of listening to a modern narrative of what can be accomplished by a woman of color, I could instead look into my roots to see the prominent roles women played and the great things they achieved. From a mental health perspective, this information is also valuable. Following your roots to the history of where you are from, may open yourself to personal development in line with that heritage. By acknowledging where you come from, you may learn where you want to go, igniting passions and awakening yourself into a new knowledge of self.

Knowing my roots, finding out the true history of where I came from enabled me to move past the rage, disillusionment and outright lies I experienced growing up and throughout my life. The purposeful mistreatment, degradation and inhumanity shown to women and people of color do not have to be your reality. Getting over the fear that is projected on to us is important in self-development. Having the knowledge that my roots and my history are rich with innovation, culture and spiritual values, enabled me to move forward with strength, and to feel proud of where I came from. As well, it reminded me of our shared history and similarities of all humans. In learning the roots of my people, my history, I was better able to reconcile the false picture I receive from mainstream media and society today. This awakening brought me further into my personal development and fueled my passion. Seeking out my personal history I was empowered to move past the perceptions of my childhood and the realities I see happening to the brothers and sisters that share my heritage, to a point where I began to understand myself more deeply, which led me closer to self-love.

TWO

THE POWER OF KNOWING

True inner knowing is a state that brings about a conscious self-love. This is self-awareness and knowledge of the soul and our purpose. Often it is difficult to achieve a higher knowledge because a variety of obstacles block our understanding of self: internal and external conflict, fear, and behavior. Overcoming obstacles is possible but there must be a conscious choice for self-love instead of agreeing with conditioned beliefs. Our selves are our souls and the power of knowing opens us up to self-love.

Growing up in the west end of Winnipeg, Manitoba, I lived in a section of the city riddled with low income struggles including poverty, violence and drugs. Since this was my reality at a young age, part of me believed this would be the way my life would progress. It was a belief that my outcomes would match my current reality; this was how people lived from my perspective. It was as though I was set out to live in the same situation for my entire life. Opportunities to change were not obvious or encouraged. On the other hand, I also felt a deeper pull in another direction. Something was telling me that there was so much more for me in the world; this was my inner knowing. An underlying passion or drive for unknown potential and possibility was weighed down by the poverty and negativity in my environment. The struggle was connecting my inner knowledge to my reality, which didn't match up.

On my journey to inner knowing I had begun to challenge my own belief systems and really examine where I derived these beliefs from. Realizing the deeply ingrained teachings I received were about competition instead of love, conformity instead of self-exploration, and memorization instead of imagination, allowed my true self-knowledge to occur which resulted in self-love. This understanding is where the real change started happening for me. The change towards loving myself enabled me to trust in the passion and purpose of who

I am, rather than a manipulated belief system. Our beliefs sometimes prevent self-love.

The messages we receive from the time we are born teach us to believe certain things as true and to compare ourselves to certain standards. Family, church, school, and media influences are handing us our belief system instead of allowing us to discover ourselves. As a unique individual, self-love will develop more naturally if you instead focus on a journey to self-awareness. Do the messages you are getting feel right? Instead of looking outward, take time to look within yourself to find this knowledge of what is true to you. It's an advancement, a spiritual awakening that gives you permission to breathe creativity into your life.

Let's take a look at what exactly beliefs are. Beliefs are formed by having an experience and then forming an opinion about that experience. The initial thought or reaction to the experience can become a belief. Once the belief thought is considered valid, evidence is collected to support the belief especially during future experiences that are similar. For example, if you are chased by a barking dog at a young age it might scare you. You form a belief that dogs are scary. Every time you encounter another dog, you anticipate it being scary which escalates the likelihood that it will happen. If a dog runs or barks, it might seem scary because you formed that opinion during your previous experience. Your beliefs are shaping your reality. After multiple incidents that prove your belief, it becomes deeply engrained in your perception and may affect your ability to truly know yourself and achieve self-love.

The essence of self-awareness or lack thereof has a lot to do with fear. What you fear and why is a big part of inner knowledge and development of self-love. One place to start is dealing with what you fear and knowing why you feel that way. By acknowledging and studying our fears we can know ourselves instead of allowing the fear to control and change our intentions. Once we have acknowledged our fears and discovered the incident or experiences that created those fears, we can move past them into self-love. The power of inner knowing brings you to love who you are. Self-discovery leads to self-love. Our fears are windows into who we are. By examining these fears and finding the experience that caused beliefs to become fears, we can open ourselves up to self-love.

The power of knowing opens us to fully immerse ourselves in discovering our passion and embracing our purpose. Once we become consciously aware we move towards self-love and truth. Instead of worrying about how others see us, we must look deeply within to find out who we are and what our soul's truth is. Ask yourself what do you know to be true about yourself? What is in conflict with this knowledge? Grab a pen and paper and jot down your answers as they come to you... I'll wait.

***

Now think about what you wrote. How does it make you feel? Are there any fears of uncertainties holding you back when you answer that question? Overcoming fears, doubts, or external factors that challenge your inner knowing is important. These external factors can potentially block your self-awareness and prohibit spiritual awakening. Who are you is not dictated by where you are, what you are or other external factors, it is only within you and it is unique to you. No one else can know you as well as you know yourself. And when you have fully discovered yourself, accept yourself and removed all preconceived notions of self you can love

21

yourself with the knowledge and truth of who you are.

Dig deep and take the opportunity to consciously choose to love you. Stop looking to family, friends and the outside environment to define who you are. Strip that all away and allow yourself to be you as you are naturally intended. If you know yourself, you get to love yourself better.

THREE

....

THE ILLUSION OF
PERFECTION

We see it everywhere; Bright women constantly chasing after the illusion of perfection. And it's even harder if they don't fall in the category of privileged Caucasian women.

Many of us chase perfection. So why do we do this? Just a few years ago I found myself in this constant state of comparing myself to everyone around me. I compared myself to my friends, family members and even celebrities. Not a day went by, when on my way to work, I looked up at the illuminated billboards showcasing women of color whose body measures were downright obscenely divine. All the women I knew seemed to be doing better at life than myself; they knew better, dressed better, loved stronger, were more passionate, did their make-up better and generally excelled at everything – being mothers, wives, professionals, love interests; the works.

But here's the thing, *NO ONE IS PERFECT!*

Many of us just give the illusion of perfection to cover up our imperfections. And slowly I came to the realization that a great deal of how we perceive others is merely a façade, something that was never there to begin with.

At some point in our lives we have adopted the concept of perfection without question and at any cost. This in itself is exhausting for everyone but can be more so for women of color who are more likely to face issues such as racism, poverty or abuse. There is an increasing marginalization of minorities in the world as people fear different cultures, races and religions and the end result is a competitive environment, where these women need to work twice as hard as their Caucasian peers and still don't receive the same recognition.

When you're a compulsive over-achiever and hold yourself to extremely high standards, this can only worsen the situation.

The journey through life is a strenuous one, but we need to remember that it starts with a single step and a single thought - that we are worthy of our own love and respect. Self-love is a conscious and soulful act, one that is not easy to achieve as you have to overcome years of social engineering that deem you not good enough because of your color or 'more likely to drop out of school' or 'make the wrong life choices'. However, it is fixable. Years of self-doubt and unrealistic expectations, where you need to strive for perfection all the time in every aspect of your life, can have a very detrimental effect on the way you perceive yourself and what others expect from you. Healthy boundaries are all about letting our loved ones, friends and colleagues know that we value ourselves as individuals and are willing to invest just as much in every relationship – business or personal – as much as the other party.

Self-love is about balancing the give and take; it's about seizing life's opportunities and never abusing yourself in the name of a relationship, a person or a goal. How many times have you heard the phrase "We all have to make sacrifices"? It's become ingrained in the way we raise children of different ethnic background to prepare them for a future, where they will always feel they need to try just a little bit harder than their Caucasian peers to prove they're 'as good', 'as capable' and 'as worthy'. As a woman of color it is hard to overlook the double standards, the unintentional glares and the ever-present racial prejudice. But you can start the healing process from within. Until you stop trying to be perfect in every aspect you will never start to feel adequate. But once you stop being apologetic, an enormous weight will be lifted off your shoulders and you will find yourself empowered to do great things.

We can only reach our true potential when we're not burdened by society's pre-conceived perception of who we're supposed to be and what we're supposed to accomplish. Your skin color does not define your path in life, your professional direction, your circle of friends, hobbies, relationships or anything else. You do. And the sense of self-love you hold for yourself because, people are drawn to love and they're drawn to individuals who know their worth, their strengths and weaknesses, but always express these with a feeling of deep appreciation for themselves as unique human beings.

When you stop trying to be perfect and start focusing on expressing what makes you...well, you – that's the moment when all illusions subside and we start living a life that is real, powerful, meaningful and authentic. Because the very pursuit of perfect is nothing more than the denial of the imperfections that make us human and it is those very imperfections that give us our unique qualities and character that make us stand out in the crowd. Do you willingly want to make yourself conform to the media-approved version of women of color? Do you voluntarily want to wipe any shade of individuality and personality that will otherwise attract people of worth in your life and not such that perceive you as a poster woman for your race? You are the only person whose opinion matters and once you fully grasp the concept of self-perception, self-love and self-realization – your life will be filled with other remarkable individuals who share the same values, dreams and passions as you. Become the centre of your universe and, surely enough, you will find other people gravitating towards your powerful core pretty soon. Because when you learn to love yourself you also learn to love humanity as a whole.

ADELINE BIRD

FOUR

....

YOU ARE WORTH IT

What does this really mean – *"You are worth it"*? You must have heard this before, maybe even repeated it to yourself, but chances are you didn't actually believe it deep down. If you did, you wouldn't feel wrong – the wrong size, the wrong weight, the wrong shape, the wrong color, the wrong class, the wrong age, the wrong smarts, the wrong ____ fill in the blank. You would feel enough, but you don't, do you?

Feeling enough is the same as feeling worth it, but we humans generally struggle with this concept. As much as men might not feel enough, women feel even less than, and as women of color, we tend to feel less than less than. There's this subtle (and sometimes not so subtle) hierarchy that society quietly reinforces for us in a million different ways, reminding us of the pecking order and what we have to do to ourselves to become acceptable.

So, as women, we shave our legs and armpits, go on diets, pluck our brows, lighten our skin, straighten our hair, push up our breasts, paint our faces, submit, shelve our dreams and ambitions because they are too big for everybody else to handle and we act small. Why? Because that's what society tells us to do so we can fit in.

We do our very best to erase what we are so we can become more like the cookie-cutter version of who we think we should be. In other words, we live a lie so we can buy approval. We allow society to make us believe that we are our hair, skin color, our clothes, the shape of our butts or our relationships. If it was possible for us to conform to this mythical standard of beauty and acceptability and magically transform ourselves into the straighter haired, lighter skinned (read 'white') image (with the perfectly small nose and perfect family of course), would we all be beautiful and live happily ever after? Nah, we'd just all be the same!

So this is the crux of the matter. If you are not tall enough, it's because you are shorter than someone else. If you are not pale enough, smart enough, thin enough etc., it's only in comparison to someone else, who might be smarter but fatter, or thinner but darker or any other number of permutations. How crazy is that? You are unique and there is great beauty in that.

The Creator don't make no junk

Whenever I think about self-worth and self-love, I think about this little gem: "I know I'm somebody because God made me and God don't make no junk." We should all read that every day. I don't remember where I saw or heard it but it turns out that Ethel Waters said it. She was something of a trailblazer for African American women. Born into poverty, abuse and neglect in 1896, Waters went from cleaning houses at age eight to being the first woman of color to star on Broadway, feature on radio, appear on T.V. and have 50 hit songs.

Whether you believe in God or not, it doesn't matter – the same sentiment applies. You are a spiritual being having a human experience and therefore you have value. If you were born, you are here, breathing and sending your energy out into the universe and that counts for something – how can you not be worthy?

Not so very long ago, women weren't allowed to vote, drive a car or hold public office and endured other restrictions that are unthinkable today. We have moved on somewhat but we still have many other lingering myths about our capabilities and worth, which will take time to dispel. It starts with you and me – we can't blame society because we are part of that same society and it's up to us to break the mold and be the new trailblazers.

Even if you don't think you are worthy, you have a responsibility to every other person on the planet to get your act together and start loving yourself. We are here to serve and you can't serve from an empty cup. So many people confuse self-love with the ego but it is more of a suspension of the ego.

Self-love is selfish and self-centered but it isn't self-involved. When you believe in yourself and accept yourself, you stop the second-guessing and the comparisons. You stop obsessing about whether you are good enough or worthy enough and you stop wasting all your energy trying to be everything that you are not. This allows you to relax into who you really are. When you give yourself permission to be you, just you, in all your glorious messiness, you can stop looking for validation from outside and you can rediscover the gift of you. Then, when you feel better about yourself, you are set free from all the confusing static and are naturally more available to help other people.

Wise Words

A wise woman once taught me one of the most profound lessons about self-love. She pointed out that when I was treating myself badly, acting small and pretending that I didn't matter, I was teaching my nieces and those around me to do the same thing. It was such an eye-opener for me.

If you have children, ask yourself what you are teaching them about how to live. This puts self-love into a whole new perspective because we all want our children to be happy, functional human beings but we got to realize that this begins with loving the self. If you can't show them how it's done, no amount of talking is going to change that.

So how do you love yourself?

The same way you love anyone dear to you - you play nice. You don't criticize, break down, mock, undermine or find fault. You are gentle, compassionate, forgiving and supportive. You give them space, you listen, you pay attention and show respect and you affirm, over and over again, by word and deed: *"You are worth it."*

WORKBOOK ONE

Before You Begin....
Create a feel good space.

With each workbook, give yourself permission to make the process significant and sacred.... I mean, learning to love yourself is quite significant and sacred, so give yourself permission to do so. This was designed for you in mind...yes you. Fully and freely write down whatever inspires you in the moment. Grab a cup of tea, turn on your favorite tunes, light a candle, smudge, get your crystals, or even say a prayer. Just create a space that allows you to feel good while you take the time to tap into your inner truth.

Your feel good space is yours to create.

Now I know many of us have busy lives. So, feel free to create a space wherever. This can be while waiting in the car for your children after school, or your lunch break, during your commute to the office.... Wherever you can create a space to consciously participate in the goodness you are about to experience.

Here we go....
What do I need to do to begin to love myself Soulfully & Consciously?

_____

_____

_____

_____

_____

_____

_____

Bridging Self-love with your soul and conscious. This is where you are going to feel your soul. You are going to explore a side of you that perhaps you may have never explored before. So here's the catch...It's going to require an open and focused heart. And yes you may cry, get angry, scream in glory, or even throw this book across the room...its ok, this is about you, and all that means is change is occurring. You're good. So feel free to swear, change your mind, put the book the book down and come back to it, add or take away, or even resist, just know with resistance comes change. This isn't an exam or a test, this is your workshop to explore your soul.

Just trust yourself.

Connect with your feelings. Breath. Take a few breaths and connect with how you feel. When it comes to loving yourself how you feel is so important. Everything we do is driven by how we want to feel, from what we eat to what we buy, there is always a feeling we want to feel, and it's always a desire to feel good. I want you to tap into that part of you...you know, that part that leads you to say things like "I just knew in my heart." Your heart, yes, that's where I need you to connect with. Tap into the feeling of happiness, joy and even the negative emotions such as anger and sadness, all come from the heart. When you feel this that's where the real work comes from and begins to manifest.

Let's begin....

KNOWING YOUR HISTORY.

There are many benefits to knowing your history, it gives birth to understanding your culture and who you are as individual.

Note: If you need to take some time to do some research please feel free to do so.

How much do you know about your history?

This can be everything from your family history, culture, traditions and ancestry roots.

_____

_____

_____

What are some the traditions or cultural practices you may still practice or are aware of? How does that make you feel?

_____

_____

_____

_____

_____

Be Unapologetically You.

What part of your history makes you feel sad, angry, frustrated?

_____

_____

_____

_____

_____

What part of your history uplifts you?

_____

_____

_____

_____

_____

Perfection...the greatest illusion. Sit. Breath. Get conscious. Let your inner truth flow.

What does perfection look and feel like to you?

_____

_____

_____

_____

_____

In what ways do you chase perfection?

_____

_____

_____

_____

_____

That critical voice in your head.... you know, that one that has you comparing yourself to others and whole lot of other issues.

What are some of the negative things that voice tells you about yourself?

_____

_____

_____

_____

_____

What feelings come up when this critical voice shows up?

_____

_____

_____

_____

_____

How is perfection getting in your way of being who you truly are?

_____

_____

_____

_____

_____

On the other hand, we also have this other voice that isn't as vocal but is loving and kind.

What does that part of you tell you about who you are?

_____

_____

_____

_____

_____

How does that kind and loving voice make you feel?

_____

_____

_____

_____

_____

Knowing yourself is your introductory to wisdom. Inner knowing creates a space for self-acceptance, creativity, wisdom and self-love.

Ask yourself, *who am I?* Take your time with this one......

How do you see yourself?

_____
_____
_____
_____
_____

What belief systems do hold about yourself?

_____
_____
_____
_____
_____

Where do these beliefs come from? I.e. Your parents, church, teachers etc.

_____
_____
_____

How have these beliefs served you in a negative way?

_____

_____

_____

_____

_____

How have they served you in a positive way?

_____

_____

_____

_____

_____

What belief systems are you willing to let go of?

_____

_____

_____

_____

_____

ADELINE BIRD

I invite you to create space to say a mantra I am going to provide. So find a quiet spot, get comfortable and relax.

Give the words the power they carry.

In 1999, a Japanese scientist by the name of Dr. Masaru Emoto released a study he conducted on water crystals and words. The results were that the crystals were always beautiful when given positive words, and when given negative the crystals became disfigured. I honestly do suggest you research his work yourself, you won't regret it.

Back to my lecture, with these findings and the understanding that our bodies are made up of 70% percent water, just think what we are doing to our bodies when we talk negatively about ourselves, this is why positive self talk is so crucial.

Say it out loud. Mean it, and if you have to say it more than once to feel it, DO IT!

Begin....

I AM AT PEACE.

I RELEASE ANYTHING AND EVERYTHING THAT NO LONGER SERVES ME.

I HAVE THE POWER, STRENGTH AND KNOWLEDGE TO BE COURAGEOUS IN MY LIFE.

I ALLOW AND WELCOME CHANGE.

I AM OPEN, AND WILLING TO CREATE NEW THOUGHTS ABOUT MYSELF.

I AM CAPABLE AND COURAGEOUS ENOUGH TO APPRECIATE AND LOVE EVERY SINGLE PIECE OF MYSELF.

SECTION TWO

....

SELF LOVE AS AN ACT OF REVOLUTION

FIVE

....

THE REVOLUTION

So much has been written about self-love, yet for most of the planet, it's not even on the horizon. Self-love remains this elusive, mysterious thing that most of us have only a slight relationship with and we've all been looking for it in the wrong places. Searching for self-love is a bit like searching for happiness and just as futile because both self-love and happiness are by-products of things like beliefs.

If learning how to love yourself is not a priority, today is the day to change that. And make no mistake about it, loving yourself is hard work. If it were easy, we would all know how to do it. When you were born, you were this perfect little being that knew exactly how to love yourself. You didn't know any different.

Then your parents, relatives, culture, schooling, the media and society at large began to leave one stamp after another, which slowly dissolved that love. Learning, unlearning, re-learning to love yourself is an opportunity to reclaim that same love we embodied as children.

As people of color we have absorbed generations of hurt and trauma. Not only do we inherit the energy, and genes from hurt and trauma, but we also inherit beliefs, values and habits that don't necessarily serve us well.

It happens to all of us, the struggle is universal. So self-love is less about learning how to do it and more about unlearning all the stuff you have collected on the way since birth that led you to believe you weren't deserving of love, particularly from yourself. I invite you to dismantle all of the beliefs that hold you back, making room for you to build new ones that support your every existence.

Why revolt to self-love?

"The revolution is not an apple that falls when it is ripe. You have to make it fall." ~ Che Guevara

A revolution is an uprising. It's a revolt against the way things are and it demands drastic, radical changes. Revolutions occur when the current status quo is no longer tolerable. The revolution of self-love is only possible with awareness and a willingness to perceive a different reality.

A revolution is fundamentally about changing. In life, you are either growing or decaying because there is no limbo - you cannot stand still somewhere in the middle and hope that things will get better by themselves.

Revolutions aren't fun. Nobody wakes up and thinks to themselves – today seems like a good day to start a revolution. No, a revolution is born from frustration and longing. It bubbles up from a place of despair and desperation when you feel there must be a better way and you are finally prepared to do something about it or die trying. And it doesn't stop there. Even after a revolution has occurred, you have to be vigilant. It becomes about making sure you don't exchange one set of rules for another.

"I love to see a young girl go out and grab the world by the lapels, Life's a bitch. You've got to go out and kick ass." ~ Maya Angelou

Why should self-love be a revolutionary act? First and foremost because learning to love yourself is your most important work. Tap into the fierce and serious you – there are no half-measures. A revolution is full-on – there is no time for wishy-washy or for sitting around hoping, wishing and praying.

This is yours. And if you're anything like me, you have always known that there has to be something bigger and greater than what has been presented to us. In my journey of personal growth, self-love has been that bigger, greater thing to me. When I first began my journey into personal development, I lacked an understanding about who I am. I forgot along the way, it got lost in relationships, from all levels from romances to friendships. I needed to back away, find myself again. And yes, my loved ones took it personally, but that's not for you to hold onto.

Self-love is ultimately a soulful declaration of your independence! It sets you free from all the things you believed made you unworthy of love. A revolution aims to overturn the old and bring in the new but that means a process of active rebuilding. It takes time and effort to construct a whole new vision for yourself but if the old one isn't working, what have you got to lose?

Loving yourself is not just for your benefit, it benefits humanity. It's not an option, a nice-to-have, an extravagance or a luxury, it's an obligation, and it's your universal right. It is part of your soul's contract. Growing up, we all get the message that love is important - we are encouraged to be good and kind to others. Nobody encourages us to love ourselves or put ourselves and our needs first because that is seen as selfish or narcissistic. In fact, self-love makes you indestructible.

As women of color, we bear the major brunt of this because historically we have been expected to be "strong". We are expected to work more for less money, make sure that we don't do anything to make people feel uncomfortable, be able to raise our children alone, and at the same time take and nurture our communities as best we can. In 2016 we are still viewed as the weaker sex, but if you look at it from a conscious stand point, you will begin to see we have had to have enormous strength, for generations upon generations. We watched our grandmothers give until there was nothing was left, we watched our mothers boldly handle both careers and family life.

Loving yourself creates space that allows you to reach your full potential, have good and satisfying relationships or pass down a positive legacy to your children. Without loving yourself, you can't break destructive ancestral cycles – like the abuse, anger and addictions that get passed down from generation to generation. Without loving yourself, you can't reveal your precious gifts to the world and share them.

Without loving yourself, you can't truly love anyone else. You are also solely responsible for loving yourself. Other people can love you of course, but it's not the same thing. Take care of you – if you don't, you can't take care of anyone else. Because at the end of the day, it all starts with you.

"And the day came when the risk to remain tight in a bud was more painful than the risk it took to blossom" ~ Anaïs Nin

The only constant we can rely on is change but the problem is that change is almost always painful. They say that pain is inevitable but the suffering is optional. Pain really is just a messenger; its only function is to get your attention. You can ignore it, repress it or try to hide it. Interestingly enough, pain does this thing, where it gets louder and louder! So loud, you can no longer ignore it.

So where does the word revolution come from? It's from the Latin word "revolver" which means to turn or roll back, and originated as a way to describe the movement of planets around the sun. Getting to self-love is also a turning back - turning back to who you really are, underneath the dross of mediocrity, labels and old, tired beliefs.

A revolution is about freedom from the shackles that hold you back. Most of the time those shackles are self-imposed. That sounds like bad news, but in fact, it's just the opposite. You can't change other people but you can work on changing yourself. And as intimidating as that sounds, it's actually a lot of fun.

ADELINE BIRD

···

SIX

THE MIRACLE OF YOU

Einstein observed that there are two ways to live your life: "You can live as if nothing is a miracle; or, you can live as if everything is a miracle." We live on a blue planet that circles around a ball of fire next to a moon that moves the sea, and you don't believe in miracles? And you are here.

Just for a minute, look at your hand. Turn it over, bend your fingers and wiggle your thumb. Did you know that there are roughly 29 bones, 29 joints, 123 ligaments, 48 nerves and 30 arteries just in that one hand? 34 muscles are devoted to moving the fingers and thumb but there are no muscles in the fingers. Instead, 17 muscles in the palm and 18 in the forearm operate your fingers from afar via tendons.

Hands can sculpt, write, paint, play a piano, button up a shirt, gently wash a newborn and karate chop through a block of wood. With enough practice, you can make them do extraordinary things but even something as seemingly ordinary as turning the page of a book takes a symphony of precision and coordination between your eye, brain, muscles and tendons. Now tell me you are not a miracle.

If you ever doubt that you are a part of the great web and mystery of life, consider that a fern, a sun flower, a sea shell, the Milky Way, hurricanes and the bones in your fingers all express the Fibonacci principle - nature's language of numbers. Yet you are a unique specimen amongst 7 billion people living on the earth! So you are different and special, just like everybody else.

Are you enough?

You are here, you exist and you breathe and that's enough. You are a spirit having a human experience and that's enough. The idea that you have to somehow prove your worth by looking a certain way, earning a certain amount or doing certain things is.... well, ludicrous if you ask me.

Divesting yourself of all the layers your family and society has piled on your head is a radical move. Now let's get over ourselves and take that first step. Ask yourself what small thing you can do today, right now, to move forward and revolutionize your life.

"The best helping hand that you will ever receive is the one at the end of your own arm. "

~ Fred Dehner

Nobody is born with hatred in their heart. We learn to hate, to be intolerant, to be racist, to feel jealousy, guilt, betrayal and fear. We learn to judge. Unfortunately, anytime you include those negatives in your energy, they bounce right back at you. In essence, we learn to play the game of life by other people's rules but when we question the validity of those rules, we break free.

When we come from a place of trying to fit in, to be accepted, to be successful, to be loved, we end up hiding our true selves and we forget how to trust ourselves. In my experience, this can automatically cause pain – how can it not when we have bought into the lie that we are not enough?

This monstrous lie is so huge and so convincing that everybody feels it at some stage of their journey. That's the great irony of being alive – you, me and every other person that has ever lived, feels or has felt at one point, that they were not good enough. It's like a cosmic joke but it's not funny until you finally get it.

So think about it for just a moment. If you don't feel good enough and chances are the next person doesn't feel good enough and the next one definitely doesn't feel good enough and the next and the next and, yes, the next, what the hell does "good enough" really even mean? Nothing. It's just a mirage. Besides, even if there were some magical measuring stick to figure out where you fit on the "good enough scale", what measurement would you use?

Pounds and ounces, dollars and cents, feet and inches? Or maybe the number of clothes in your wardrobe would make you measure up or your job or your husband's job. What about the number of friends you have, your hair, your shoe size or the length of your eye lashes? See how ridiculous this all is? Whichever way you look at it, it's all completely arbitrary because none of this really matters in the slightest. It only matters when you think it does and when you actually stop to question it, none of it is important.

"Don't be afraid to go where you've never gone and do what you've never done, because both are necessary to have what you've never had and be who you've never been." ~ Mike Dooley

Look at it this way - you might not be smart but the smart person might not be fast. The fast one might not be pretty but the pretty one might not be strong. The strong one might not be articulate but the articulate one might not be creative. We could go on like this all day. You cannot be all things at once, but you can be you. You can only be you. The trap is in comparisons. The second you compare yourself to anybody else, you set yourself up for either feeling a false sense of superiority or an equally false sense of inferiority.

When we look at other people, we judge the way they dress, the shape of their nose, their teeth, the color of their skin, their weight, their hair, how they speak, the car they drive, and on and on. Oh my God, what are we doing? If we judge others, it means we can be judged. If we exclude others because of judgment, it means that we can be excluded too. Now there's a big can of worms.

The human race is not a club with membership criteria, we all belong. Self-love then is as much a revolution of surrender as it is of change. The change occurs in your thinking and in questioning your beliefs, but you have to surrender yourself completely to who you are by accepting your imperfections. So many people see their differences as hardships and the reason why they are not happy, successful or confident. Our differences are our strengths, or could be if we allowed them to be. A muscle only gets stronger by being pushed and stressed and so it is with the human spirit.

Eckhart Tolle says *"Life will give you whatever experience is most helpful for the evolution of your consciousness. How do you know this is the experience you need? Because this is the experience you are having at this moment."*

Surrendering to who you are frees you to take risks and step out of your comfort zone. Until you do that, you are stuck with wasting your energy fighting yourself because you constantly view the world through your insecurities, anxiety, fear and anger.

Schooling and education? Big differences between the two. Schools have this tendency to teach conformity, rather than how to live life to the fullest. We are taught how to obey, follow the rules, color between the lines and how to be a compliant citizen. It steals the one thing it takes so much work to get back, which is your childhood curiosity, and crams you full of facts and information that you will probably never use. They reward you for memorizing stuff through standardized testing that treats everyone as if they were all cut from the same cloth.

"'Normal' is getting dressed in clothes that you buy for work and driving through traffic in a car that you are still paying for – in order to get to the job, you need to pay for the clothes and the car, and the house you leave vacant all day so you can afford to live in it." ~ Ellen Goodman

Above all, they teach you how to consume by perpetuating the myth that success, happiness and all that is good and holy rests in getting those grades. Critical thinking, inquiry and the sheer joy in the process of learning are the casualties. What you learn becomes more important than what you gain from learning it. That is not education.

When you leave school, you are automatically programmed to think you must go to college so you can get a good job, get married, buy a house, have the 2.4 children that you will push through the same system and then work until you retire, when you can supposedly do what you want and finally be happy right? Millions of people do this and are they happy? Not even close. Some people are happy with this and there is nothing wrong with that. Many, many people, however, feel trapped in a world that feels suffocating and they die without ever realizing their dreams or knowing that there is more.

Don't be one of those. Educate yourself so that you can be more than a cookie-cutter product of what society tells you that you should be. At some point, you have to wake up and see through the illusion of "fitting in" and the illusion of "normal". That's why it's a revolution – you are taking the concept of the "norm" and burning it because there is no normal! The so called "normal" we have been sold is a bill of goods – it's a big con to get you tied up in debt and misery while you dutifully consume and consume in the never ending and fruitless search for happiness through possessions and status.

We have whole industries that profit from making us feel insecure about the way we look, what we buy and how we choose to live. From the color of our hair to the width of our bums to the car we drive, advertising dictates what's in and what's out. These industries depend on us using all these external measures to gauge how successful or happy we should be.

It's manufactured perfection of course to get us to conform to this size, shape, skin color, height, wealth, image, blah blah – but as so few of us fit into that narrow little box, should we be trying to squeeze ourselves into it anyway? Hell, no! Make your own box or better yet, get rid of the box altogether.

So here's the thing – if you are "ugly" in whatever way you think you are, your job is to love yourself so much that other "ugly" people can look at you and think "Hey, I can do that too". Everyone's definition of their ugliness is different (that should give you a huge clue!) Some might concentrate on the physical, others on the financial and still others on the relationship aspects. Whatever your perceived downfall, your job is to love and accept yourself no matter what.

Your job is to shine so much light around that it illuminates the path for the rest of us. You have to love yourself because of your perceived weaknesses and flaws and not in spite of them.

Blaze your own trail, be your own person and stake your claim to all the oxygen, happiness, life, success, joy and peace you can get. Live your life on your terms. Viva the revolution!

"There is no greater gift you can give or receive than to honor your calling. It's why you were born."

-Oprah Winfrey

And then you can help someone else find their way. What is a gift for if not to share? Your gifts are not for you alone; they are for everyone else. When you pass those gifts on, however, your life is enriched because that is why we are here – for connection and to find out that we are all in this together. Our differences make us what we are and trying to be a clone of what advertising is selling us is selling out. Don't buy it, not even for a second.

"You are a child of the universe, no less than the trees and the stars; you have a right to be here."

~ Max Ehrmann

....

SEVEN

BOUNDARIES

"You are not required to set yourself on fire to keep other people warm"

Part of the revolution of self-love is this small question of boundaries. A boundary is your definition of what you will accept and what you won't accept.

Brené Brown puts it nicely: *"A boundary is simply what's okay and what's not okay."*

So many of us have a fuzzy conscious concept of what "okay" means but if we learn to listen the small voice of intuition, we know.

You can't know what okay signifies until you claim your identity. If you don't have boundaries, it means you have no identity or at least no clear definition of that identity. You don't know where you and your responsibilities end and where other people and their responsibilities begin. You haven't figured out "you" yet and that's a large stumbling block on the way to self-love.

Now this may seem at odds with the notion that we are all connected but it isn't. You still have a responsibility to uphold your end of the bargain as a soul expressing itself in human form. As a unique spark of divinity, you still need to claim that divinity and you have to allow others to do the same. You can share parts of your journey with other people but you can't travel the exact same road.

When you do for others what they should rightly be doing for themselves, you rob them. You rob them of the lessons they will learn by trying, failing and getting up to try again. You rob them of the joy of self-discovery. You also rob them of independence. Women are especially guilty of this. We have been conditioned through the ages to be the caretakers, often at our own expense.

. At the root of an inability to set boundaries is fear – fear of upsetting people if you say no, fear of not being able to cope with their disappointment, fear of them not being able to cope without your help, fear of offending people, fear of not being loved, fear of being disliked, fear of being judged, fear, fear, fear.

Saying no makes you uncomfortable, just like standing up for yourself does, especially if you haven't had any practice at it or if you had no role models who could show you how to do it. If you experienced witnessing the women around you allow people to walk all over them, chances are those women simply couldn't teach you what they didn't know, and you have probably learned that allowing this type of energy into your life is normal.

It takes enormous courage to fight through the inertia of this kind of comfort zone because if it is behavior that you have practiced all of your life, it's unconscious and has become your "normal". As such, you don't think about it, it's not even on your radar screen.

I grew up witnessing my mother being abused by a particular boyfriend. In fact, from what I know of my biological father he was a pretty abusive man himself. I knew in my heart that this was not okay. But in turn as I got old enough to be in a relationship, I began to tolerate the same behavior. I spent years in abusive relationships. From physical to verbal...I've been there. It became normal, so normal I became comfortable in it.

The funny thing about a comfort zone is that it isn't that comfortable, it's just the level of discomfort you have come to expect. What you might not have considered is that saying yes when you mean no comes at a much higher price than being honest with yourself and saying no. You see, the temporary discomfort of stepping out onto that scary ledge where your needs actually matter is nothing compared to the ongoing discomfort of continually denying those needs. When you allow someone to abuse you, physically, mentally, emotionally or in any other way, the inevitable outcome is resentment. Resentment is a form of chronic anger, which simmers, festers and lingers.

Resentment literally means "to feel again", which means it doesn't go away and you are stuck with the poison. That's not good for you or anyone else. Getting roped into something you don't want to do is not generosity or kindness. If you don't want to do something and go ahead and do it anyway, out of cowardice or a sense of obligation, expect to feel powerless and resentful.

On the other side of the coin, only when you have your boundaries in place can you be truly generous and compassionate because your actions and intentions are pure – they are not clouded by all the negativity that gets wrapped up with the "shoulds". Without boundaries, life is very messy and confusing.

One of the most powerful questions I have ever been asked was *"Would you want to teach this _____ (fill in the blank) to your daughters?"*

It doesn't matter if you have children or not, the question still stands. We all want to pass something on to the next person, the next generation or future generations. We all want to believe that our lives counted for something. When you take yourself out of the equation and ask whether what you are doing is acceptable for someone else to do, it puts a whole different spin on things. Here is where you get the full import of how what you do, say and think affects not only you, but everyone else.

Not stepping into your identity and your power is unacceptable. There, I said it. Not claiming your creative ability to shape your world is selfish. You may think "Who am I to do something great, different, special, amazing...?" My question is – who are you not to? Seriously, who gives you the right to hide under a bushel?

"I need to be startlingly clear. This thing of finding your authentic voice, expressing your blessed weirdness and revealing your soul isn't an elegant process. You don't do it to be cool.
It's only real when it is ruthless, relentless and inevitable. But it is also a matter of personal and collective survival. Yes, it's that important. You are that critical."
~ Jacob Norby

TURN FAILING INTO A LEARNING OPPORTUNITY

There are two sides to the boundary issue – the one side is the enormity and difficulty of setting personal boundaries and the other side is realizing that there are no boundaries or barriers preventing you from being whatever you want to be. One of the biggest barriers to this is the fear of failure.

Failure is inevitable, get used to it. Failure, however, is not bad and it is nothing to be ashamed of at all but is an opportunity for you to learn something. If you think you can escape failure by not attempting anything, you have already blocked yourself from the beauty of learning. Failure is made out to be the boogeyman but it's merely feedback. Nothing more, nothing less. It tells you to do things differently or to do different things. If you have never failed, it means you have never fully tried.

"Sometimes your only available transportation is a leap of faith" ~ Margaret Shepard

Loving yourself requires putting yourself on the line and taking risks. A risk is inherently uncertain – you might win but you might lose. Kind of like how I felt about producing this book, I was resistant to writing this book, because I felt it might offend people. Either way, you need to have the self-confidence to prevail. Confidence is an interesting word – it means "firmly trusting, bold" and "to have full trust or reliance". Now you can't trust yourself until you have gone out there and tried. This doesn't mean that everything you touch must turn to gold, it just means that you try and that whatever the outcome is, you keep going. If the outcome is good, you chalk it up to experience and keep doing that. If the outcome is bad, you chalk it up to experience and do something else.

"What if I fall? Oh, but my darling what if you fly?" ~ Erin Hanson

ADELINE BIRD

WORKBOOK TWO

CELEBRATE THE REVOLUTION OF YOUR SOUL

Things may get a little heavy in this section. Transformation isn't always comfortable, and when the discomfort arrives, the urge to resist persist. There are ways to get past that urge.

Go on a date with change. Your life is your art. And art creates evolution and with evolution comes change. If you're anything like me, day one of creating change in my life is easy, its day 4 or 5 when the tension starts to kick in and I'm not feeling it anymore, and that's the challenge of change. Here's what I've learned, from a biological stand point, that change is literally asking your cells to change its shape.

So what's the secret behind getting past those feelings of resistance? Allow me to enlighten you...

Breathe Deep. In through your nose and out through your mouth. When resistance begins to rear its head where it's not needed, take a moment to stop and breathe.... Deeply

Give yourself permission to change. Remind yourself that resistance is cause for celebration, because all it means is transformation is happening!

Self-Edit. Go back, revise, edit, erase. As I mentioned earlier, your life is your art. So whether we imagine it as a painting or writing, the point is there is room for editing through getting clear about why change needs to occur.

PUT SOME RESPECT ON YOUR TRUTH

We all do it. We deceive ourselves into thinking certain circumstances, situations and things will bring us happiness and freedom. When we deceive ourselves we create space for self-discovery, naturally we fall into doing things for reasons we may not understand. It's about getting real with the misunderstandings of ourselves. Respecting that at times we do things for the wrong reasons, even if it doesn't feel that way at first. Get connected with your truth, however that may look or feel. Open up your heart.

The self-love revolution consists of reflection. In this exercise I invite you to get yourself a mirror or turn on the cell phone camera to selfie mode and say the following to yourself....

I am deserving of......
I am deserving of love

Say this a few times to yourself. If you are using your cell phone get bold record yourself and watch. Notice how you feel.

Now, try the doing the same thing, except this time say to yourself, I am _____ (Fill in the blank)

I am love, I am abundance. *What type of feeling comes to you when doing this exercise?*

_____
_____
_____
_____
_____

Check in with your body, *how does it feel?*

_____
_____
_____

Is this all true to you? Why or why not?

_____

_____

_____

_____

_____

THE MIRACLE OF YOU

What did you learn about who you are as a child?

_____

_____

_____

_____

_____

How did that make you feel?

_____

_____

_____

_____

What teachings about yourself did you take with you into your adulthood? Which of those teachings continue to serve you and which ones do a disservice to your adulthood?

_____

_____

_____

_____

_____

We crave the feeling of being able to love ourselves fully. We make conscious decisions to create changes in our lives so we can get there. And then it happens....

The voice.

Yes, the voice. You know her. That critical, and negative voice, that asks you *"Who do you think you are?"*

Ugh. Let's take this revolution one step further...

Your critical self. Criticism slowly but surely breaks down your soul. Let's examine and begin to change the critical you.

What do you criticize yourself for? List 5 things.

What do you criticize others for?

Is there a connection between what you criticize yourself for and others? If so, why do you think that is?

Be Unapologetically You.

What do you get celebrated for?

_____

_____

_____

_____

_____

What do you celebrate others for?

_____

_____

_____

_____

_____

What connection exists between what you celebrate about yourself from others?

_____

_____

_____

_____

_____

And there you have it! Another break through!

BOUNDARIES

As I mentioned earlier, loving yourself requires creating boundaries. Let's connect with that.

What does it mean to have a boundary to you?

_____
_____
_____
_____
_____

What type of relationship boundaries do you struggle with?

_____
_____
_____
_____
_____

For example, with myself, I struggled with boundaries when it came to romantic relationships.

Setting limits.

What are some of your limits?

Setting boundaries can be difficult if you don't know where you stand. Take into consideration what you can tolerate and accept, as well as what makes you feel uncomfortable.

THE POWER OF TURNING "SHOULDS" INTO "COULDS"

As I mentioned in this chapter, when we lack boundaries, we tend to fall into the negativity of "shoulds." This exercise will help you see the power of turning those should into coulds!

I SHOULD.........
I SHOULD BE PATIENT.

Let's turn those should into coulds....and go!

I COULD......
I COULD BE PATIENT.

Ta da! *Now how amazing does that feel?* You may find that you were "Shoulding" on yourself for something you may have never had any interest in to begin with!

SECTION THREE

....

SELF LOVE AS
A CREATIVE ACT

EIGHT

....

FORGIVE AND LET GO

You are the author of your own story. You get to write the chapters and choose the direction and it's entirely up to you, which way it goes. You literally 'make' your life, moment to moment by your choices. Even not making a choice is a choice not to make a choice.

Emily Maroutian expresses this beautifully:

> "Energy is the currency of the universe. When you 'pay' attention to something, you buy that experience. So when you allow your consciousness to focus on someone or something that annoys you, you feed it your energy, and it reciprocates the experience of being annoyed. Be selective in your focus because your attention feeds the

energy of it and keeps it alive. Not just within you, but in the collective consciousness as well."

So let's start with the creative act of forgiveness.

Forgive and Let Go

Let's be real, learning how to forgive kind of sucks. Even though we all might know, deep down, that we need to forgive so we can move on, we all tend to hang on to the pain, the injustice and the unfairness of being wronged and hurt in some way. Intellectually, you might recognize that not forgiving is poisoning your life, but emotionally, you might still be attached to reliving the initial trauma and want to have some sort of revenge or closure. You know you are hurting yourself but can't quite seem to move beyond it.

For many of us, we think that by somehow making the other person suffer, you will feel better but entertaining such thoughts makes only one person suffer and that's you. Trust me, I've done this more than 100 times. Whatever happened or didn't happen, whatever someone did or failed to do, is in the past.

Nothing can change it. The best revenge is to move on and have a happy life.

For years, I chased a man who never really loved me (and ladies we all do this at some point in our lives). He would leave, come back, leave come back......you get the picture. Each time he came back my emotions started to move towards resentment, which is not a good place to be. It wasn't until I made up my mind and decided I couldn't do this to myself anymore, and to really come to terms that it wasn't him, it was me? It was a big blow to my ego. And eventually I had to learn to not only forgive him, but forgive myself.

Lack of forgiveness keeps you locked in an ego-dominated prison of your own making. All the while you can't forgive, you are hanging on to the notion that you are different, separate and superior to the person you won't let off the hook. This, of course, is an illusion. Your ego is not your friend and all it wants is to keep things exactly as they are. There is no growth in stagnation.

Mandela, after being imprisoned by an apartheid government in South Africa for 27 years, famously said upon his release: "As I walked out the gate that would lead me to my freedom, I knew that if I didn't leave my bitterness and hatred behind, I'd still be in prison." It has been said that if you don't forgive, you become what you hate. That's really something to think about! When you forgive, you simply withdraw your precious energy from the situation, which means you can spend your energy better elsewhere.

Forgiveness then, is freedom! It's freedom from reliving the pain and the anguish that you are constantly rerunning in your head. It's freedom from the judgement, accusations and chronic anger that lingers as resentment. Resentment might feel good, empowering and justified in the moment but it is a poison that erodes your self-esteem, health and relationships.

As a type of anger, resentment makes you feel in control but it paradoxically makes you powerless because you desperately need the other person or the world at large to change in order for you to feel better. You want them to apologize, make amends, do something to undo the past or better yet, suffer as much as you have suffered. This is never going to happen so you wind up going around and around in circles and defeating yourself in the process.

Let it go. Your suffering does not make the other person suffer.

What forgiveness isn't

Forgiveness does not mean condoning or forgetting, letting the person know that what they did or didn't do was ok or any kind of reconciliation. It is none of these - it simply means releasing yourself from the grip of reliving all the bad things that might have happened to you and the need to apportion blame. And this is the crux of forgiveness – it has nothing to do with the other person or persons who might have done you wrong. You forgive for you and that's it.

The problem is, we tend to perpetuate the crimes we ascribe to others by talking about them to our friends or ruminating about them, complaining about them and generally keeping them alive. In other words, we want things to be different and therein lies the problem. You cannot rewrite the past and make it change but you can rewrite your story about the past. It can't and won't change, so stop surrendering your happiness to it.

How to forgive

This is the big question – how do you do this? How do you forgive the unforgivable? How do you move past abuse, betrayal and neglect? It's hard.

According to Fred Luskin, Director of the Stanford University Forgiveness Projects, the largest interpersonal research project ever conducted, hanging on to hurts is like having an existential tantrum. "We think the world owes us," he says. "But it doesn't. Babies die when they're born. Women are raped. Whole ethnic groups are wiped out. There's no such thing as fair. The guy who loses a parking space to a more aggressive driver thinks, 'I want that parking space.' A mother whose child has been murdered thinks, 'I want my child to be alive.' Either way, that's sometimes just not how it works."

It may seem outrageous to compare losing a parking place to being raped or losing a child but to Luskin, it's all "content" – the way we interpret such events. In your mind, your interpretation is fact, it's the way things happened. No one is disputing what happened to you but you have to realize that your emotional version of what happened is hurting you.

You have to accept that it is what it is and no matter what has happened, it's a done deal and move on from there. This is where most of us get tripped up when we think that our troubles are so much bigger and so much more important than anybody else's so we have to hold on to them.

Maybe your parents were abusive, your partner cheated on you, your sibling swindled you out of your inheritance, your friend betrayed you, you were treated like dirt because you happened to be black – it's all relative. That's not to say the experiences weren't horrible and indefensible, they were, but they happened. Life isn't fair and we have to accept that.

Luskin says there are only two steps to forgiveness, you grieve and then you let go. You are absolutely allowed to grieve - write it down, articulate it, explain it to yourself, rage about it and get it out there. Say what you need to say about how awful it was and mourn. But don't unpack and stay there. If you do, you are sacrificing far too much energy, time and headspace to things you cannot change.

The next step after the grief is releasing it all, which is simple but not necessarily easy. The way around it is to be mindful of the present and put your attention on gratitude. Gratitude is huge. In his book 'Forgiveness for Good', Luskin defines forgiveness as *"the experience of peace and understanding that can be felt in the present moment."*

Gratitude

Gratitude focuses on the present, which is all we really have. When you refuse to forgive, you keep dragging yourself back to a painful past. Bringing your attention to the now, for what you have, what you are and what you can be is a powerful creative act that can remake your world. Even if you can't find much to be grateful about, it's the search that counts. Looking for things to be grateful about primes your brain towards the positive, which means that searching for things to be positive about in the future gets easier. Anger and resentment do the opposite – they prime your brain to look for what's wrong in your life.

Perhaps the biggest gift of forgiveness is that it gives you a sense of actual control, not the false sense of control from anger. You get to decide how you will live your life, what decisions you will make and the relationships you will form without all the messy noise from the emotional pain that you once carried.

How forgiveness helps you

What you might not have considered is that forgiving others helps you deal with your own flaws and allows you to forgive yourself. We all have lingering doubts about our worthiness but until you can forgive the transgressions perpetrated by other people, you can't really forgive yourself for your own mistakes. Forgiveness opens up your heart to another way of looking at life. It's like a two-way street – if you are kinder to others, you can be kinder to yourself.

Besides that, forgiveness transforms your physical and psychological well-being. It lowers blood pressure and stress levels, improves your relationships with other people and yourself, helps with depression, anxiety and anger and allows you to be more optimistic. It also ensures that you won't suffer so much hurt in the future when things don't go as planned. Forgiving makes you more resilient and flexible in the face of life's inevitable disappointments.

It's a win-win situation - forgiveness wipes the slate clean, so to speak, so that you can have a fresh start. Lily Tomlin said *"forgiveness means giving up all hope for a better past."* Forgiveness can't be passive, like self-love can't be – you have to be fierce and apply radical forgiveness so you can get some peace and move on.

NINE

....

EMBRACE YOUR
AUTHENTIC SELF

"We have calcium in our bones, iron in our veins, carbon in our souls, and nitrogen in our brains. 93 percent stardust, with souls made of flames, we are all just stars that have people names." ~Nikita Gill

Who are you? What are you like deep down? Do you even know? These are all hard questions to answer if you have been living life on someone else's terms. There is no shortage of advice as to how to live your life but none of that matters if it doesn't fit you. Knowing who you are and what you want are oftentimes much more difficult than knowing what you don't want. So start from there.

Living an authentic life requires scraping away all the limitations you have allowed yourself to believe – like the one that whispers in your ear *"You're not good enough"*.

Unfortunately, it also requires risk and the very real possibility that people won't like you without the mask. This, in turn, requires the courage to be vulnerable, to fail, to make mistakes and to be seen – warts and all.

Having courage is not the same as being fearless. Courage is feeling the fear and the anxiety and going ahead and doing it anyway. Courage is an interesting word because the root is the Latin 'cor', meaning heart. So courage is not bravery as such but living from the heart by doing what you know in your heart is right. When you live courageously by following your heart, you conquer fear and that gives you more confidence in your own abilities to overcome life's challenges. The word confidence comes from the Latin 'con' (with) and 'fidere' (to trust or have faith in).

So living your truth leads to having more faith in yourself, which in turn leads to more courage and more confidence. It all starts with BEING authentically you, which allows you to DO what your heart calls you to do and then you HAVE the life you desire because you start to manifest the opportunities that are in alignment with your heart.

If confidence means with full trust, you have to recognize that trust is never a given. Trust has to be earned! And you earn your own trust by consistently behaving in accordance with your own values – in other words by being authentically you. The flip side to that is living a lie, which gets you distrust, doubt and uncertainty. Everyone is an original and you don't need the approval of anyone else but yourself.

As scary as authenticity is, the flip side is much scarier. Trying to be someone or something that you are not, is incredibly draining. Trying to live up to the expectations of others whilst ignoring your own aspirations is tough. Trying to maintain the wrong sense of self and a false identity is exhausting because it takes an awful lot of energy. When you attempt to be someone different to who you really are, there will naturally be loads of internal conflict. How can it be any other way? You can't not be you, you can only fake it. As there is only one you, you have no choice but to honor that you, accept it and embrace it.

So here's the problem – we live in a society that endorses and encourages non-authenticity. Social media is fabulous but it also allows people to present all the highlights of their lives and skip over the low points. You can be as selective as you like without being dishonest, except by omission. Advertising and the general media add to this by constantly fostering idealized images of beauty, acceptability and success, which makes us compare ourselves to others.

"To be nobody but yourself in a world which is doing its best, night and day, to make you everybody but yourself means to fight the hardest battle which any human being can fight and never stop fighting."

~ E. E. Cummings

When you compare yourself to someone else and feel that you come up short, you are denying your uniqueness and the things that make you special. You are rejecting your individuality and then you start to fit in and to pretend. As most of the world is pretending, putting on, shamming and presenting their unauthentic selves to the world, you are comparing your life to ones that simply don't exist! Even if someone is being authentic, you have no idea what challenges that person has faced to get there, what it cost them and how much work it took.

"Envy is ignorance; imitation is suicide."
~Emerson

So just stop the comparisons and put your energy into finding your own voice. The source of all our pain and discomfort is the notion that we are not good enough and we only feel that way by comparison. So really, you have no choice but to be you, the real you. Nobody does you like you do.

Being authentic is admittedly intimidating. On top of that, it's not a once-off, you have to commit to it over and over again. It's something you have to do and keep doing by constantly checking in with yourself and asking *"Do I really want to say/be/do this?"* This takes awareness.

"I had no idea that being your authentic self could make me as rich as I've become. If I had, I'd have done it a lot earlier." ~Oprah Winfrey

When I first started podcasting and really putting myself out there, I realized I was creating an opportunity to really live in my authentic self. This is what people wanted. And to be honest it was scary. Why? Well, I went from a school system to a working system that required me to act and be a certain way, which usually didn't speak to who I really was.

There are no 'shoulds' to living an authentic life because only you know how that looks for you. You create your life from the inside out by your thoughts, beliefs and dreams but you are not your thoughts, beliefs and dreams because these things can change. The thinker, believer and dreamer does not change however. You are allowed to change your mind, in fact it's mandatory. You can think different thoughts today from the ones you thought yesterday and contradict yourself and then do it again tomorrow.

If you follow the crowd and conform, you are not allowed to change your mind – your mind is changed for you and then you have to stay there. Trust yourself to entertain a different perspective and to change that perspective when necessary to let in new ideas and new creations.

Imposter syndrome

"I have written eleven books, but each time I think, 'Uh oh, they're going to find out now. I've run a game on everybody, and they're going to find me out.'"
~Maya Angelou

A lot of very capable and effective people are convinced that they are faking it, even when they are successful. They live in fear of being exposed as frauds. You would be absolutely amazed at how many people feel like frauds, especially women and even more so, women of color. From college students to mothers, professionals, CEOs and successful actors and authors, men and women all over the world think that one day someone will find out they are not really talented, they don't know what they are doing, they shouldn't be doing their jobs and they don't really belong there.

And it gets worse – the higher up you go and the more successful you become, the more you can feel like an imposter because you realize there is still so much more for you to learn and the goal posts are always moving. This extends beyond the workplace though. Some people feel like they are just playing house when they give a dinner party or that they aren't really grown up when "adulting".

"Good judgment comes from experience, and a lot of that comes from bad judgment." ~Will Rogers

The imposter syndrome is wide spread and the truth is that everybody is winging it to some degree so we can all calm down. Nobody is perfect and nobody knows how to do something they haven't done before so if your job is in any way challenging, there is always going to be some trial of your abilities. We don't get lessons in how to live life, have a kid, launch a business or get old. Only experience can teach us these things but the things are constantly changing. This includes yourself.

When I first launched my podcast titled Soul Unexpected, I came face to face with my version of the imposter syndrome. Let me tell you that syndrome has voice. I remember sitting behind the mic while interviewing a guest and hearing a voice in my head say, who the heck do you think you are? Who's really going to listen to what you or guests have to say? Excuse my vulnerability but I also felt that way with this book!

Everything you do is an act of creation as life is a creative process – the question is are you creating something you want or **something** you don't want? The only way to get good at something is to apply yourself, make mistakes, learn from them and try again. If you think that talent is fixed, that you should just know how to do stuff, you hold yourself back unnecessarily. When you realize that talent has to be nurtured and grown and that there will be an endless learning curve, you allow yourself to grow.

"The most common way people give up their power is by thinking they don't have any." ~Alice Walker

Instead of trying to cure the imposter syndrome, recognize it as a normal and natural feeling and welcome it because it means that you are self-aware. The minute you think you know it all is the minute you start to stagnate. Why try harder or try doing things differently if you believe you have already "arrived"? The tension generated by not knowing if you can do something well or at all is very often just the impetus you need to push yourself a bit harder to overcome the challenges and to stretch yourself beyond your current capabilities.

It might sound counterintuitive but sometimes you just have to drop your standards, stop being so hard on yourself and let go of trying to be perfect. This means you accept that you are inherently flawed and that it's ok! Then you can relax a bit, step into the real you and bring forth your unique gifts instead of burying them under a bushel of procrastination. Learn to live with the certainty of uncertainty.

ADELINE BIRD

TEN

....

TRUST THE PROCESS

Everything takes time, especially a work of art and you have to look at your life as a work of art. It's a creation but a life-long creation.

Give time some time is awesome advice, however it's sometimes hard to follow in our instant gratification society. We want it all and we want it now but life simply doesn't work that way. If your life is your own creation, then transforming it is a creative process and as such, it doesn't happen overnight. It's also a process that is ongoing and you never really get it done.

Living a life of self-love is a gradual and unfolding where you discover more and more layers with more and more meaning. At the same time, you shed the labels you have previously used to define yourself. As each layer reveals itself, you understand more about yourself and your place in the world but you are still limited by the next layer.

Think like a gardener, work like a carpenter.

In the "Little Book of Talent" Dan Coyle says you should "think like a gardener, work like a carpenter...Think patiently, without judgment. Work steadily, strategically, knowing that each piece connects to a larger whole."

Gardeners are patient. They prepare the soil, plant the seeds, water them and then nurture them while they wait patiently. The seeds have to first pass from dormancy to germination, then unfold and start to grow at their own pace. Gardeners don't expect a fully formed plant to spring instantly from the seed and they know that you can't hurry them or make them grow at your pace and that some seeds don't take at all.

Think of your growth to self-love in the same way – as something that needs to be nurtured and cultivated with patience. Prepare the ground and plant your seeds but don't get frustrated when you don't' get instantaneous results.

Carpenters need to measure and plan with precision before they cut wood and start building. They also need to practice their skills over and over before they can hope to be any good. If they rushed in without having honed their craft first and without the requisite planning, it would all be wasted effort.

So work steadily at building your cabinet of self-love. Make sure it is well-made – strong, sturdy and balanced. Know, however, that it's going to take plenty of practice, rehearsals and iterations before you come close to getting it right. Know also that sometimes it will feel like you are failing but that's all part of the trip.

Say Yes!

Yes is a magical word but one that we are used to saying to other people and shy about using with ourselves.

SAY YES TO YOU
SAY YES TO SELF-LOVE
SAY YES TO BEING FREE
SAY YES TO THE WHISPERING OF YOUR HEART
SAY YES TO JOY
SAY YES TO YOUR DREAMS

Listen to your dreams and no matter how fantastic and outrageous they seem – say yes! If not, why not? Do your dreams scare you? Good, say yes anyway. Do you think you don't have the talent to make them come true? Say yes anyway and cultivate the talent. Say yes and start looking for ways to make them happen. Start small but for goodness sakes, say yes.

Ellen Johnson Sirleaf, the 24th and current President of Liberia, said, *"The size of your dreams must always exceed your current capacity to achieve them. If your dreams do not scare you, they are not big enough."*

Don't fall for analysis paralysis where you can argue yourself out of pursuing your goals. Just say yes dammit – jump and a net will appear. It's called a leap of faith. People on their deathbeds often regret the things they didn't do, the chances they didn't take, far more than the things they did do. When you are dithering about making the right choice, always go with your heart. So many people are terrified of making the wrong choice but as none of us has a crystal ball we can't know all the answers in advance. In truth, there are no right or wrong decisions, only actions.

Make a decision and then make it right by committing to it. You will be surprised at what you call forth into your life when you do that. If you make a decision and then spend your time second-guessing yourself, you will only attract the negative consequences of that energy.

Have you ever wondered where these dreams of yours come from? They come from deep within and they are there for a reason. Remember what courage means – living from the heart. Your dreams are your personal and private invitation to claim your greatness and they are calling to you. Once you say yes and you own them and claim them, you open up a channel that allows your talents to come to the fore – talents you possibly didn't even know you had. You will be able to dig deep into resources you didn't know were there all along.

You can all expand into facing whatever life throws at you if you give yourself the chance. You find yourself when you are forced beyond your comfort zone and then you learn how powerful and amazing you really are. You know this already, by the way, but you probably don't recognize it.

What does saying yes to yourself do for you? It confirms that you are worth it. It gives you the seal of approval – from you to you. It affirms life. It inspires action, even if you are afraid. It makes you move forward instead of stagnating in the same place. It opens up new possibilities. It kindles anticipation and appreciation. It ignites passion. It helps you look to the future instead of dwelling on the past. Such a bounty from one little word.

If you are anxious about saying yes but you know you want to, try saying "I'm excited!" instead. Anxiety and excitement feel pretty much the same physiologically – rapid heartbeat, sweaty palms, surges of cortisol - but excitement is way more positive than anxiety. Excitement is expansive but anxiety is limiting. Excitement can change your mindset from dread to opportunity seeking and the situation seems less threatening.

So say yes to the new you. Say yes to the opportunities that present themselves, say yes to life. Once you accept this new way of being, loving yourself a bit more each day and loving your life, say yes.

What have we learnt here? The most important lesson is that loving yourself is no walk in the park. It doesn't come easily or naturally so you have to be fully committed and uncompromising about it. Love knows no half measures and if you want to love yourself, you are going to have to work at it.

The next is that self-love is fundamentally an act of self-awareness. It's getting to grips with where you come from and the expectations that arose from your personal history and the collective history of your tribe. It's examining the validity of every belief, feeling, emotion, idea, opinion, impression and perception that you have ever had and being willing to let it go. It's questioning every thought to find out if it is true.

With awareness comes the necessity for being truly yourself with no apologies, excuses or pretenses. This takes enormous courage because whilst conformity is stifling, it is also much safer than putting your authentic self on the line.

Self-love is the soulful, conscious, revolutionary and creative act of rewriting your story. This means letting go of the judgements, hatreds, complaints and grievances. It's the recognition that what you do for one, you do for all. When you forgive others, you can forgive yourself.

Finally, self-love is a decision but the only sane one to make if you want a stab at having a happy and fulfilled life in a seemingly insane world. Only when you love yourself can you offer the world your unique gifts. So loving yourself is your gift, to yourself and everyone around you.

WORKBOOK THREE

The Art of Letting Go

As you dive into this exercise, I invite you to take a deep breath, and as you begin to exhale allow whatever tensions that you have to leave your body. Relax your jaws, forehead and mouth.

Are you feeling relaxed? Take note of the change that has occurred in your body and how much you hold onto in your body, understand that what you hold in your body is what you hold in your mind.

Sit comfortably and say this mantra out loud to yourself.

"I am willing to release all that does not serve me. I let go, I release all tensions, fears, anger, sadness and any limiting beliefs. I am now free to let go of any thoughts, feelings and emotions that do not serve me."

Go over this section as many times as you need. Consciously letting go is a challenge.

So if any thoughts of difficulty come up, keep practicing until this exercise becomes a part of you. Once you get used to implementing this in your life, you will be able to become fully relaxed in any circumstance.

Forgive. Self-check!

When it comes time to forgive do you say things like......

"What they did is unforgivable."

"Because of them my life is ruined."

"I will never forgive them!"

Do you resonate with any of these statements?

Let me start off by saying, don't give anyone that much power over you, and secondly this section of the workbook is for you!

Forgiveness Mantra

In this practice I invite you to either sit or stand in front of a mirror and say to yourself, "I am willing and able to forgive." Breathe deeply.

I want you to take notice of how you're feeling when you say this. Do you feel stuck and unable to forgive? Or do you feel open and able? Release any feelings of judgement towards yourself.

Pay attention to how you feel.

Let's explore family attitudes towards forgiveness. Get your pen and paper out, it's time to get deep!

Was your mother forgiving?
How did or didn't she express forgiveness?

_____

_____

_____

_____

_____

Was your father a forgiving person? How did or didn't he express forgiveness?

_____

_____

_____

_____

_____

How did your family unit handle hurt and pain? How has that affected how you deal with hurt and pain today?

_____

_____

_____

_____

_____

How do you practice forgiveness?

_____

_____

_____

_____

Is the way you forgive serving or not serving you?

_____

_____

_____

Reminder: Forgiveness is done from the heart... yes, I know that sounds cheesy but it's true.

Many of us tend to view forgiveness as an "Us Vs. Them."

Let's be real, some of the people we need to forgive may have passed onto the spirit world.

In this section I invite you to make a list of 4-5 people you want to express forgiveness to.

1)
2)
3)
4)
5)

Now let's get uncomfortable for a minute and do more talking to ourselves......

I want you to imagine sitting in front of the person or people who have hurt you, let them pass through your mind, open your eyes and begin speaking to them. Tell them how you feel, whether it be *"you hurt me dearly, I am willing to forgive you and set you free."*

You may feel a little resistance, and maybe only able to forgive one or two people, and that's okay. As you keep practicing this exercise you will begin to feel the burdens fall away. Feel it.

Lastly, learn to forgive yourself. Stop being so hard on yourself. Always keep in mind, we do the best that we can do!

Embracing your authentic self.

Learning the art of embracing your authentic self takes time, patience and most importantly, practice for yourself and those around you.

What authenticity is not.

Authenticity is not saying something just because it came to your mind in the moment. Given your opinion when not needed is not authenticity, even if your opinion is right, Uncle Chris with the bad hair does not need your opinion, unless he asks.

What authenticity is.

It's about knowing yourself and becoming self-aware, it entails telling the truth without laying out all your laundry for everyone to see.
Here are a few questions to ask yourself when it comes to your authenticity......

Do you share your struggles and fears openly?

_____

_____

_____

_____

Can you admit when you have made a mistake without judging or blaming others?

_____

_____

_____

_____

When someone asks for your opinion do you tell them everything that's on your mind?

_____

_____

_____

_____

Three ways to create an authentic life.

1) Learn to function with an open mind. Ask questions, read or do a little research and explore other perspectives.

2) Get uncomfortable. Learn to admit you lack knowledge in a certain area, or that something makes you feel awkward or afraid.

3) Lastly, and most importantly, know what you value and want. Sit alone with our thoughts. This will create space for you to explore what brings you joy or what doesn't bring you joy. Get to know yourself away from people and things.

If it helps, write it down! I have said it before and I will say it again, Writing is magic!

Just. Say. YEEEEES!

Because, why not! Write down everything you desire to say yes to, for example;

I SAY YES TO LOVE!
I SAY YES TO HAPPINESS!

ELEVEN

....

SELF LOVE AS A PRACTICE

Turn on your light, it's time to go love yourself, your life and the world! Here's what I know about continuously cultivating self-love and I have faith it will be very useful in Self-Love your practice.

1. Plan Your day, week, month and even year by connecting with your inner self. *What do I need to do to maintain my self-love? What can I do this day, month, or year to generate my self-love?*
2. Take your self-love practice seriously. Loving yourself is no joke. Journal. Write things down. Writing is magic. When you wake up in the morning, set out your intentions on how you want to feel about yourself. For example: Today I choose to feel Sexy, bold and BEAUTIFUL! You get

the picture. And at the end of the day write down how you felt about yourself throughout the day, and in the am, reflect and repeat.

3. Talk to someone on the same or similar journey as you. This is important. Every single successful person, from Oprah to Will Smith has one single message in common.... and it's to surround yourself with people who are going to uplift and elevate you.

4. Listen to positive content. One way I love to fuel my soul is through podcasts, such as my own titled Soul Unexpected, which is available on Itunes and Stitcher, download and subscribe today! (Yes I just shamelessly promoted my podcast). I also love listening to motivational videos on YouTube, and audio books while I am cooking and cleaning my house. I also find yoga and meditation to be very positive.... why? Because your listening to yourself in these practices. Give it a try.

5. Lastly, GIVE! Go do something nice for someone you know or don't know WITHOUT expectation. When you give, it's literally an exchange of energy.

When it Storms....

Let's be real, shit happens. You are going to have moments of feeling disconnected with your soul. Life happens and OMG!! You feel like life couldn't get any worse... well, here's the thing, accept it.

Refrain from resisting the moment. Fully dive into it so you can fully uncover the truth behind the experience. Be present.

Reflect on this book. Go back and revisit everything you wrote down. Go back to the chapters that really helped you transform. Read it out loud. Read it until that feeling slowly comes back to your DNA.

CLOSING TREATMENT

YOU ARE MORE THAN YOUR NAME.
YOU ARE MORE THAN YOU SKIN COLOR.
YOU ARE A DESCENDANT OF ROYALTY.
TREAT YOURSELF THAT WAY.

MAKE IT A DECLARATION!

I AM LOVE.
I AM LIGHT.
I AM PROSPERITY.
I AM CREATIVITY.
I AM ENOUGH.
I AM WORTH IT.

I AM SO STRONG THAT NO ONE CAN DISTURB
MY PIECE OF MIND.

ADELINE BIRD

ABOUT THE AUTHOR

My first dance with self-love as an adult began when I was able to step outside my comfort zone. When ambition meets freedom, and consciousness makes love to revolution, magic begins.

I was brought here by my love for personal development, creativity, entrepreneurship and a purpose for elevating women and women of color.

With a background in social work, my life's mission has always been to help others find their inner most creative self through self-love.

Thank you for having me in your space, it was a slice.

With Love,
Adeline xoxo

ADELINE BIRD

Made in the USA
Las Vegas, NV
10 July 2021